JUN 1 0 2014

First-Person Histories

DIARY OF CHARLOTTE FORTEN

A FREE BLACK GIRL

BEFORE THE CIVIL WAR

by Charlotte Forten

CAPSTONE PRESS
a capstone imprint

Fact Finders are published by Capstone Press,
1710 Roe Crest Drive, North Mankato, Minnesota 56003
www.capstonepub.com

Library of Congress Cataloging-in-Publication Data
Cataloging-in-publication information is on file with the Library of Congress.
ISBN 978-1-4765-4196-9 (library binding)
ISBN 978-1-4765-5139-5 (paperback)
ISBN 978-1-4765-5988-9 (eBook PDF)

Editorial Credits
Michelle Hasselius, editor; Bobbie Nuytten, designer; Wanda Winch, media researcher; Laura Manthe,
production specialist

Photo Credits
The Bridgeman Art Library: Private Collection/William Henry Bartlett, 11; Courtesy of Clipart ETC,
Florida Center for Instructional Technology, USF, 13; CriaImages.com: Jay Robert Nash Collection,
14, 15; Getty Images: The Bridgeman Art Library, 25, Buyenlarge, 26; Library of Congress: Prints and
Photographs Division, 9, 19, 29; Moorland-Springarn Research Center, Howard University, cover (right,
portrait left), 1, 4, 5; North Wind Picture Archives, 7, 8, 10, 16, 17, 21, 22 (bottom), 27; Shutterstock:
Andrzej Sowa, cover (bottom left), Katya Ulitina, cover (hand writing background), pearl7, 22 (top),
Picsfive, (ripped paper design), Sergey Galushko, 20, Svitlana-ua, 18

Printed in the United States of America in Stevens Point, Wisconsin.
092013   007769WZS14

TABLE OF CONTENTS

A Free Black Girl
Before the
CIVIL WAR

Charlotte Forten recorded her first journal entry at the age of 16 in May 1854. She had recently left her father's home in Pennsylvania to live and attend school in Salem, Massachusetts. This chance to learn in a public school was a rare opportunity for a free African-American during the period of slavery.

In the 1850s most African-Americans living in the United States were slaves. Northern states did not allow slavery but southern states did. Owners could treat their slaves as they wanted. Very few slaves received an education.

Charlotte grew up in the North with friends and family who spoke out against slavery. Her mother, Mary Virginia Forten, was a founding member of the Philadelphia Female Anti-Slavery Society. She died when Charlotte was 3 years old. Charlotte continued to live with her father, Robert Forten, in the free state of Pennsylvania after her mother died. Charlotte's father worked in the family's successful sailmaking business and was an **abolitionist**.

Charlotte Forten's diary entry from July 23, 1863

In 1854 even free states and territories in the United States did not allow African-Americans to go to school with white students. **Segregation** forced free African-Americans to set up their own schools. Funds for these schools were limited. African-Americans often struggled to pay for books and school supplies.

Charlotte's school in Salem taught African-American and white students together. She had the same chance as white students to receive a good education. Charlotte lived with Charles and Amy Remond in Salem. Charles, the son of free black parents, was active in the movement against slavery. Amy was like Charlotte's second mother.

Charlotte was more fortunate than most African-Americans of her time. She received a good education. Friends and family inspired Charlotte to use her knowledge to help other African-Americans. Charlotte's own words tell about her struggles as a free African-American in the 1800s.

portrait of Charlotte Forten Grimke

abolitionist—a person who worked to end slavery

segregation—the act or practice of keeping people or groups apart from one another

THE Diary OF Charlotte Forten
1854

Wednesday, May 24, 1854—

Rose at five. The sun was shining brightly through my window, and I felt **vexed** with myself that he should have risen before me; I shall not let him have that advantage again very soon. How bright and beautiful are these May mornings! The air is so pure and balmy, the trees are in full blossom, and the little birds sing sweetly. I stand by the window listening to their music, but suddenly remember that I have an Arithmetic lesson which employes me until breakfast; then to school, recited my lessons and **commenced** my journal. After dinner practised a music lesson, did some sewing, and then took a pleasant walk by the water. I stood for some time admiring the waves as they rose and fell, sparkling in the sun, and could not help envying a party of boys who were enjoying themselves in a sailing boat. On my way home, I stopped at Mrs. [Caroline] Putman's and commenced reading "Hard Times," a new story by [Charles] Dickens … I anticipate to much pleasure in reading this story.—Saw some agreeable friends … prepared tea, and spent the evening in writing.

Charlotte's diary entries appear word for word as they were written, whenever possible. Because the diary appears in its original form, you will notice misspellings and mistakes in grammar. To make Charlotte's meaning clear, in some instances, corrections or explanations within a set of brackets follow the mistakes. Sometimes text has been removed from the diary entries. In these cases, you will notice three dots in a row, which are called ellipses. Ellipses show that words or sentences are missing from the text.

the harbor in Salem, Massachusetts, around 1870

vex—to annoy or irritate

commence—to begin something

Thursday, May 25, 1854—

Did not intend to write this evening, but have just heard of something that is worth recording ... Another **fugitive** [Anthony Burns] from **bondage** has been arrested; a poor man, who for two short months has trod the soil and breathed the air of the "Old Bay State," [Massachusetts] was arrested like a criminal in the streets of her capital, and is now kept strictly guarded,—a double police force is required, the military are in readiness; and all this is done to prevent a man, whom God has created in his own image, from regaining that freedom with which, he, in common with every other human being, is **endowed**. I can only hope and pray most **earnestly** that Boston will not again disgrace herself by sending him back to a bondage worse than death; or rather that she will redeem herself from the disgrace which his arrest alone has brought upon her. The weather is gloomy and my feelings correspond with it ...

Runaway slave Anthony Burns was captured in Boston, as shown in this illustration from the 1850s.

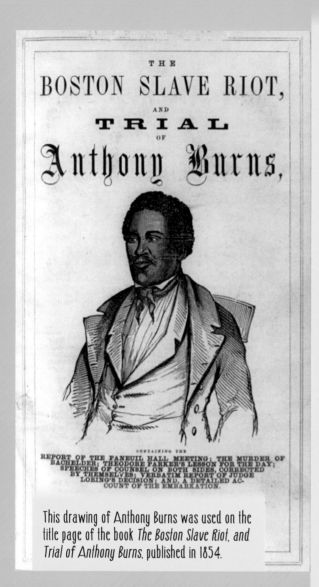

THE
BOSTON SLAVE RIOT,
AND
TRIAL
OF
Anthony Burns,

CONTAINING THE
REPORT OF THE FANEUIL HALL MEETING; THE MURDER OF
BACHELDER; THEODORE PARKER'S LESSON FOR THE DAY;
SPEECHES OF COUNSEL ON BOTH SIDES, CORRECTED
BY THEMSELVES; VERBATIM REPORT OF JUDGE
LORING'S DECISION; AND, A DETAILED AC-
COUNT OF THE EMBARKATION.

This drawing of Anthony Burns was used on the title page of the book *The Boston Slave Riot, and Trial of Anthony Burns*, published in 1854.

Anthony Burns and the Fugitive Slave Act

In 1854 a runaway slave named Anthony Burns escaped from the slave state of Virginia. He was captured in Massachusetts, which was a free state. Burns was arrested after his capture. He was tried under the Fugitive Slave Act.

The Fugitive Slave Act allowed slave owners to search for runaway slaves in free states. Captured slaves were returned to their owners. This act also made it illegal to help slaves escape to free states. Anyone who took care of or hid runaways could be fined $1,000 and jailed for six months. Many free African-Americans moved to Canada to avoid the punishments of the Fugitive Slave Act.

Abolitionists opposed the Fugitive Slave Act. People came to Boston by the thousands to protest Burns' arrest. They tried to help Burns escape but failed. Boston police officers and armed soldiers surrounded Burns at his trial to prevent his escape. Burns was returned to his slave master after the trial. In less than a year, abolitionists paid for his freedom and Burns returned to the North.

fugitive—someone who is running away from the police

bondage—to keep a person as a slave

endow—to provide a quality or talent

earnest—serious

Saturday, May 27, 1854—

Have been very busy all morning, sweeping, dusting, sewing, and doing **sundry** other little things which are always to be done on Saturday.—Spent a delightful hour in the afternoon at Miss [Mary] Shepard's ... Returned home, read the Anti-Slavery [news]papers, and then went down to the depot to meet father; he had arrived in Boston early in the morning, regretted very much that he had not reached there in the evening before to attend the great meeting at Faneuil Hall. He says that the excitement in Boston is very great; the trial of the poor man [Anthony Burns] takes place on Monday. We scarcely dare to think what may be the result; there seems to be nothing too bad for these northern tools of slavery to do.

This illustration of Boston Harbor was used at the top of *Gleason's Pictorial*, a local newspaper, in 1854.

People opposed to Anthony Burns' arrest attended a meeting at Faneuil Hall in Boston, shown in this drawing from the 1800s.

Friday, June 2, 1854—

Our worst fears are realized; the decision was against poor Burns, and he has been sent back to a bondage worse, a thousand times worse than death. Even an attempt at rescue was utterly impossible; the prisoner was completely surrounded by soldiers with **bayonets** fixed, a canon loaded, ready to be fired at the slightest sign. To-day Massachusetts has again been disgraced; again has she showed her submissions to the Slave Power; and Oh! with what deep sorrow do we think of what will doubtless be the fate of that poor man, when he is again consigned to the horrors of slavery. With what scorn must that government be regarded which cowardly assembles thousands of soldiers to satisfy the demands of slaveholders; to deprive of his freedom a man, created in God's own image, whose sole offense is the color of his skin! And if resistance is offered to this outrage, these soldiers are to shoot down American citizens without mercy; and this by express orders of a government which proudly boasts of being the freest in the world ... I can write no more. A cloud seems hanging over me, over all our persecuted race, which nothing can **dispel**.

bayonet—a long knife fastened to the end of a rifle

dispel—to put an end to something

Boston citizens were angry over the court's ruling to return Anthony Burns to slavery, as shown in this illustration from 1895.

Sunday, June 4, 1854—

A beautiful day. The sky is cloudless, the sun shines warm and bright, and a delicious breeze fans my cheeks as I sit by the window writing. How strange it is that in a world so beautiful, there can be so much wickedness, on this delightful day, while many are enjoying themselves in their happy homes, not poor Burns only, but millions beside are suffering in chains; and how many Christian ministers to-day will mention him, or those who suffer with him? How many will speak from the pulpit against the cruel outrage on humanity which has just been committed, or against the many, even worse ones, which are committed in this country every day? Too well do we know that there are but very few, and these few alone deserve to be called the ministers of Christ, whose doctrine was 'Break every yoke, and let the **oppressed** go free.' ...

This reference is from a Bible verse from the book of Isaiah, chapter 58, verse 6.

Nearly 4 million slaves worked on southern plantations in the 1850s.

oppressed—to be treated in a cruel, unfair, and harsh way

People clashed with abolitionists over anti-slavery views, as shown in this drawing from 1860.

Saturday, June 10, 1854—

Received two letters, one from father. The other from Annie [Woods Webb]. Letters from home! how eagerly expected, how gladly welcomed they are! To my great disappointment, father has decided not to remove to New England. He is, as I feared he would be, much prejudiced against it on account of the recent slave case, or, he says, he is so against Boston, and I think he intends that feeling to the whole state at least. I shall write to-morrow, and use every argument I can think of, to induce him to change his opinion. I do not wish to have my long-cherished plan of our having together a pleasant New England home, defeated ...

1831 masthead of *The Liberator*, an anti-slavery newspaper

THE LIBERATOR.

VOL. I.]   WILLIAM LLOYD GARRISON AND ISAAC KNAP[P]   [NO. 22.

BOSTON, MASSACHUSETTS.]   OUR COUNTRY IS THE WORLD—OUR COUNTRYMEN AR[E]   1831.

Saturday, June 17, 1864—

A bad headache has prevented my enjoying the fine weather to-day, or taking as much exercise as I generally do. Did some sewing on my return from school.—Read the "Liberator," then practised a music lesson. Late in the afternoon I went to Mrs. Putnam's, and listened to an account of her journey, and her visit to my home—home I must still call it, though I may never live there again; yet while those I love are there, it shall be "home, sweet home." ... In the evening Miss Sarah Remond read aloud Mr. Frothingham's sermon, whose stern truths shocked so many of his congregation. We, of course, were deeply interested in it, and felt grateful to this truly Christian minister for his **eloquent** defense of oppressed humanity. While Miss R.[emond] was reading, Miss Osborne came in, and said she believed that we never talked or read anything but Anti-Slavery; she was quite tired of it. We assured her that she could never hear anything better; and said it was natural that we should speak and read much, on a subject so interesting to us ...

The liberator was an anti-slavery newspaper published in Boston from 1831 to 1865. This newspaper was printed to convince people that slavery was wrong. The liberator had a strong impact on many people and helped start the abolitionist movement.

Sunday, June 25, 1854—

Have been writing nearly all day.—This afternoon went to Anti-Slavery meeting in Danvers, from which I have just returned. Mr. [Andrew] Foss spoke eloquently, and with that warmth and sincerity which evidently come from the heart. He said he was rejoiced that the people at the North were beginning to feel that slavery is no longer confined to the black man alone, but that they too must wear the yoke; and they are becoming roused on the subject at last ... As we walked home, Miss [Sarah Parker] Remond and I were wishing that we could have an anti-slavery meeting in the neighborhood every Sunday, and as well attended as this was. But it is now quite late, every one has retired to rest except myself. It is time that I should do so, as I wish to rise before the sun.

In this drawing from the 1850s, abolitionist Wendell Phillips speaks at an anti-slavery meeting in Boston.

eloquent—smooth and clear in expression

Saturday, July 15, 1854—

Have been very busy to-day.—On my return from school did some sewing, and made some gingerbread.—Afterwards adopted "Bloomer" costume and ascended the highest cherry tree, which being the first feat of the kind ever performed by me, I deem worthy of note.—Obtained some fine fruit, and felt for the first time "**monarch** of all I surveyed," and then descended from my elevated position ...

Monday, July 17, 1854—

... I have seen to-day a picture of a dear old English church ... Oh! England my heart yearns towards thee as to a loved and loving friend! I long to behold thee, to dwell in one of thy quiet homes, far from the scenes of my early childhood; far from the land, my native land—where I am hated and oppressed because God has given me a dark skin. How did this cruel this absurd prejudice ever exist? how can it exist? When I think of it a feeling of **indignation** rises in my soul too deep for utterance. This evening I have been thinking of it very much. When, Oh! when will these dark clouds clear away? When will the glorious light of Liberty and Justice appear? The prospect seems very gloomy ...

monarch—someone who rules over a kingdom, such as a king or queen

indignation—a feeling of righteous anger

18

The Bloomer costume was popular among women in the early 1850s, as shown in this drawing from 1851.

Amelia Jenks Bloomer and the Bloomer Costume

Amelia Jenks Bloomer was a women's rights activist who lived from 1818 to 1874. Bloomer thought it was unfair that women were expected to wear the uncomfortable clothes of the mid-1800s. At that time women wore heavy, floor-length dresses over many underskirts. They also wore tight corsets around their waists and rib cages to make themselves look thinner. Corsets made moving and breathing difficult.

Bloomer began the style of wearing loose pants under a knee-length skirt. This outfit was called the Bloomer costume. When wearing the Bloomer costume, women could climb trees and ride bicycles. Women stopped wearing the Bloomer costume by the mid-1850s.

Friday, July 28, 1854—

This morning Miss Creamer, a friend of our teacher, came into the school. She is a very learned lady; a Latin teacher in Troy Seminary, and an authoress ... She seems to be a very nervous and excitable person, and I found myself frequently contrasting her appearance with that of our dear teacher, who looked so perfectly calm and composed ... we felt very happy to hear her say afterwards that she was much pleased, and thought we did very well. I do think reading one's composition, before strangers is a trying task. If I were to tell Mrs. R.[emond] this, I know she would ask how I could expect to become what I often say I should like to be—an Anti-Slavery lecturer. But I think that I should then trust to the inspiration of the subject.—This evening read "Poems of Phillis Wheatley," an African slave, who lived in Boston at the time of the Revolution. She was a wonderfully gifted woman, and many of her poems are very beautiful. Her character and genius afford a striking proof of the falseness of the assertion made by some that hers is an **inferior** race.

inferior—lower in rank or status

Phillis Wheatley

Phillis Wheatley was born in Africa in 1753. At age 7 she was captured by slave traders and sold in Boston to the Wheatley family.

John Wheatley recognized Phillis' intelligence and taught her to read and write. Within 16 months Phillis had learned the English language and went on to study Latin and Greek.

When she was about 13 or 14 years old, Phillis was writing complex poetry. Some of her poems were published in newspapers. Many people did not believe that a slave wrote the poems.

In 1773 Phillis traveled to England with the Wheatleys. There she published her first book, *Poems on Various Subjects, Religious and Moral*. Phillis was the first African-American woman from the United States to write and publish a book.

Phillis Wheatley as a young girl

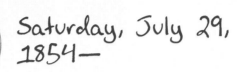

Saturday, July 29, 1854—

This afternoon went to the pastures with Sarah R.[emond], Helen P.[utnam Gilliard], and the children to gather blackberries. There was a delightful breeze, and I must confess that I felt more inclined to sit on the rocks, and admire the beautiful prospect, than plunge among thorns and briars in search of berries,—to the great annoyance of Frank, who declared that I "should never get any berries, stopping every minute to look at the clouds and rocks as if I had never seen any before." After picking for some time, we came to a pleasant grove, and seating ourselves on the moss-covered rocks greatly enjoyed our lunch, and the delightful, rural spot in which it was taken. We returned home just as the sun was setting, and although we had not a great many berries, and felt rather tired, we all agreed that our "berrying" had been a very pleasant one.

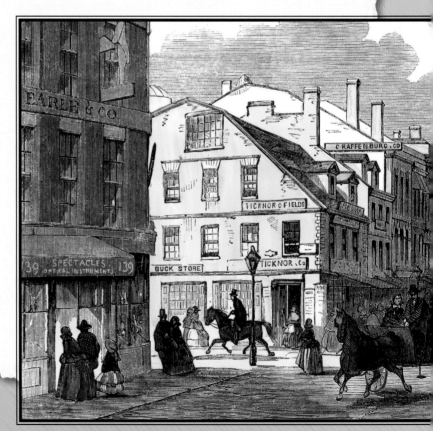

Tuesday, August 1, 1854—

To-day is the twentieth anniversary of British emancipation. The joy that we feel at an event so just and so glorious is greatly saddened by thoughts of the bitter and cruel oppression which still exists in our own land so proudly claiming to be "the land of the free." And how very distant seems the day when she will follow the example of "the mother country," and liberate her millions of suffering slaves! This morning I went with Mr. and Mrs. R.[emond] to the celebration at Abingdon. The weather was delightful, and a very large number of persons was assembled in the beautiful

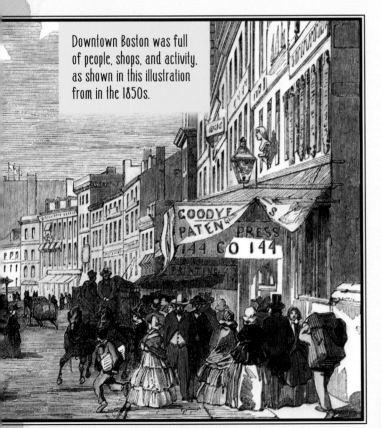

Downtown Boston was full of people, shops, and activity, as shown in this illustration from in the 1850s.

grove ... On returning home we stopped in Boston and passed some time very pleasantly in the Common listening to the music which enlivened the stillness of the sultry night. It was quite late when we reached home. And I returned to rest feeling that this has been one of the happiest days of my life, and thinking hopefully of the happy glorious day when every **fetter** shall be broken, and throughout this land there shall no longer be a single slave!

On August 1, 1834, the Slavery Abolition Act ended slavery in all of Great Britain's colonies. Emancipation Day is still celebrated in Great Britain during the first week of August.

fetter—a chain or metal rings locked around the ankles of a slave or prisoner

Thursday, August 17, 1854—

My birthday—How much I feel to-day my own utter insignificance! It is true the years of my life are but few. But have I improved them as I should have done? No! I feel grieved and ashamed to think how very little I know of what I should know of what is really good and useful. May this knowledge of my want of knowledge be to me a fresh incentive to more earnest, thoughtful action, more persevering study! I trust, I believe it will ...

Friday, August 25—

Our usually quiet city has been quite noisy for the last two days with the drums and other accompaniments of the military.—I shall be thankful when their "**muster**" is over. I never liked soldiers, and since the disgraceful capture of poor Burns, they are more hateful to me than ever ...

muster—to come together

24

Wednesday, September 27—

Have just received a letter from father, which contains a very unexpected summons.—I must return home next month.—It would give me much pleasure to see the loved ones there. But I cannot bear to think of leaving Salem, now that I have just begun to learn. Most earnestly do I wish to possess what is most invaluable,—a thorough education. I will write immediately and use every argument to induce father to permit me to remain a little longer.—I feel as if I *cannot* go now. Oh! I do hope that father will consent to my staying.

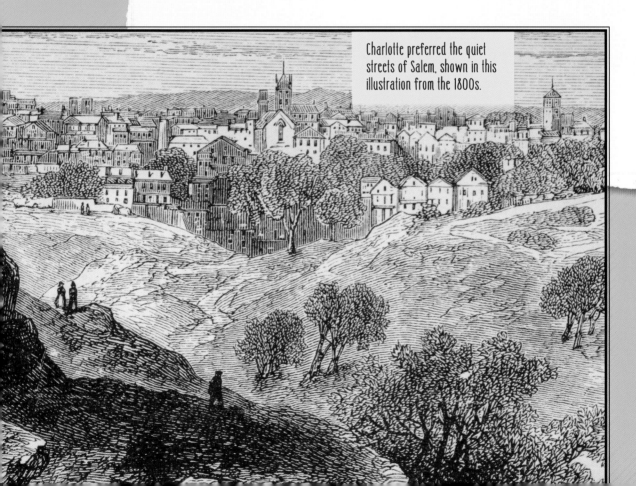

Charlotte preferred the quiet streets of Salem, shown in this illustration from the 1800s.

Only some African-American children got the chance to go to school, like this girl shown studying in this 1899 photograph.

Tuesday, Oct. 3—

This afternoon I had a lesson in teaching.—I heard the recitations of the third and fourth classes—we got along very pleasantly, and one pretty, rosy-cheeked little girl told me afterwards that she liked me *very* much for a teacher ...

Monday, October 23—

At last I have received the long expected letter, which to my great joy, contains the eagerly desired permission to remain. I thank father very much for his kindness, and am determined that so far as I am concerned, he shall never have cause to regret it. I will spare no effort to become what he desires that I should be; to prepare myself well for the responsible duties of a teacher, and to live for the good that I can do my oppressed and suffering fellow-creatures ...

Charlotte was excited to become a teacher. In this illustration from the 1870s, a new teacher is interviewed by a school board.

Eyewitness to U.S. History

Charlotte's wish to become a teacher came true. In June 1856 she accepted an offer to teach in the Epes Grammar School, and became the first African-American teacher in Salem.

Slavery in the United States officially ended with the adoption of the 13th Amendment to the U.S. Constitution in December 1865. After the Civil War (1861–1865), most former slaves in the South still farmed for a living. Many worked for their old masters, but they were free. They received wages or a share of the crops they grew in exchange for their labor.

Charlotte believed that education would bring African-Americans equality. She was one of the first African-American teachers to help educate the children of former slaves. She taught reading, writing, spelling, history, and math in a one-room schoolhouse in Port Royal Sound, South Carolina. In 1878 Charlotte married Francis Grimke. Charlotte died on July 22, 1914, in Washington, D.C.

Timeline

- Dates in Charlotte Forten's life
- Important dates during slavery in America

1840
Charlotte's mother, Mary Virginia Forten, dies.

1837
Charlotte Forten is born in Philadelphia.

1838
A white mob burns an orphanage for African-American children in Philadelphia.

—1835 — 1840

1854

President Millard Fillmore signs the Fugitive Slave Act. Anthony Burns is captured and tried in Boston.

1863

U.S. President Abraham Lincoln declares the Emancipation Proclamation. This presidential order said that all slaves in the United States were free.

1914

Charlotte dies in Washington, D.C.

1854

Charlotte begins writing in her journal.

1861

The Civil War begins.

1878

Charlotte marries Francis Grimke.

1856

Charlotte graduates from Salem Normal School and receives her first teaching position at Epes Grammar School in Salem.

1865

The 13th Amendment ends slavery.

1855

1865

Glossary

abolitionist (ab-uh-LI-shuhn-ist)—a person who worked to end slavery

bayonet (BAY-uh-net)—a long knife fastened to the end of a rifle

bondage (BON-dij)—to keep a person as a slave

commence (kuh-MENSS)—to begin something

dispel (diss-PEL)—to put an end to something

earnest (UHRN-ist)—serious

eloquent (EL-uh-kwuhnt)—smooth and clear in expression

endow (in-DOW)—to provide a quality or talent

fetter (FET-ur)—a chain or metal rings locked around the ankles of a slave or prisoner

fugitive (FYOO-juh-tiv)—someone who is running away from the police

indignation (in-dig-NAY-shuhn)—a feeling of righteous anger

inferior (in-FEER-ee-ur)—lower in rank or status

monarch (MON-ark)—someone who rules over a kingdom, such as a king or queen

muster (MUHS-tuhr)—to come together

oppressed (oh-PRESST)—to be treated in a cruel, unfair, and harsh way

segregation (seg-ruh-GAY-shuhn)—the act or practice of keeping people or groups apart from one another

sundry (SUHN-dree)—various

vex (VEKS)—to annoy or irritate

Read More

Aloian, Molly. *Phillis Wheatley: Poet of the Revolutionary Era.* Understanding the American Revolution. New York: Crabtree Publishing Company, 2013.

Herr, Melody. *The Slave Trade.* World Black History. Chicago: Heinemann Library, 2010.

Meadows, James. *Slavery: The Struggle for Freedom.* Journey to Freedom. Mankato, Minn.: Child's World, 2009.

Critical Thinking Using the Common Core

1. On June 25, 1854, Charlotte wrote, "... The people at the North were beginning to feel that slavery is no longer confined to the black man alone, but that they too must wear the yoke." What does Charlotte mean by this? How do you think slavery affected people living in the free states of the North? (Key Ideas and Details)

2. Some schools in the northern states were segregated during Charlotte's time. What does segregation mean? Using what you know about American history, describe how segregation ended in the United States. (Integration of Knowledge and Ideas)

3. Charlotte began working as a teacher in Port Royal Sound, South Carolina, around 1862. What other events were going on in America during this time? Use the timeline to help you with your answer. (Craft and Structure)

Internet Sites

FactHound offers a safe, fun way to find Internet sites related to this book. All of the sites on FactHound have been researched by our staff.

Here's all you do:

Visit *www.facthound.com*

Type in this code: 9781476541969

 Check out projects, games and lots more at
www.capstonekids.com

Index